GREENHOUSES, LIGHTHOUSES

ALSO BY TUNG-HUI HU

Mine (2007)

The Book of Motion (2003)

Tung-Hui Hu

GREENHOUSES, LIGHTHOUSES

COPPER CANYON PRESS

PORT TOWNSEND, WASHINGTON

Printed in the United States of America

Cover art: Doug and Mike Starn, *Attracted to Light 1 (ephemera)*, 1996–2004. Toned silver print on Thai mulberry paper, 3.5 x 7.5 inches. Artists Rights Society (ARS), NY.

page viii: L. Dudley Stamp, et al. *Land Utilisation Survey of Britain*. Sheet 99, Pembroke and Tenby. Map, 1:63360. London: Geographical Publications, 1935. (Original in National Library of Scotland.)

page 2: John Cary. *Cary's New Map of England And Wales, With Part Of Scotland*. Sheets 19-20. Map. London: John Cary, 1794. (Original in David Rumsey Historical Map Collection.)

page 20: *Ordnance Survey of Great Britain, New Series*. Sheet 9. Map, 1:63360. Southampton: Ordnance Survey Office, 1904. (Original in British Library.)

page 26: L. Abbe Diquemare and Louis Stanislas d'Arcy Delarochette. *A chart of the British Channel and the Bay of Biscay, with a part of the North Sea, and the entrance of St. George's Channel*. Map. London: William Faden, 1794. (Original in David Rumsey Historical Map Collection.)

Copper Canyon Press is in residence at Fort Worden State Park in Port Townsend, Washington, under the auspices of Centrum. Centrum is a gathering place for artists and creative thinkers from around the world, students of all ages and backgrounds, and audiences seeking extraordinary cultural enrichment.

LIBRARY OF CONGRESS CATALOGING-IN-PUBLICATION DATA

Hu, Tung-Hui, 1978–
  [Poems. Selections]
  Greenhouses, lighthouses / Tung-Hui Hu.
     pages cm
  Includes bibliographical references and index.
  Poems.
  ISBN 978-1-55659-406-9 (paperback : alk. paper)
  I. Title.

  PS3608.U22G74 2012
  811'.6—dc23

2012039153

98765432 first printing

COPPER CANYON PRESS
Post Office Box 271
Port Townsend, Washington 98368
www.coppercanyonpress.org

for E.E.B.

ACKNOWLEDGMENTS

Grateful acknowledgment is made to the editors of the publications in which poems from this book first appeared: Boston Review, The Concher, Crazyhorse, CURA, The Drunken Boat, Gastronomica, Guernica, Kenyon Review Online, Meridian, Michigan Quarterly Review, Narrative, Ninth Letter, The Pinch, Yalobusha Review.

Thanks to the many lovely friends and readers over the years who helped these poems along; in particular, Twilight Greenaway, Megan Pugh, and Tonaya Thompson lent their keen editorial eyes to this project. Thanks also to Hawthornden Castle, the MacDowell Colony, the Michigan Society of Fellows, Millay Colony, the University of Mississippi, Ragdale, the Virginia Center for the Creative Arts, and Yaddo for offering me the time to write and, occasionally, the time to nap.

You did not sail in the broad-benched ships.

Stesichorus, *Palinode*

CONTENTS

3   Invisible Green

8   Ars Poetica

9   Exposure

10   History of Pornography

11   Ode, Washington Dulles International Airport

13   What Was Rationed

14   On Curing Images and Pork

15   Cosmos Revealed behind a Dense Curtain of Poppies

16   The Order of Things

17   Year of Following People

18   Gleaners

19   Hands and Feet

21   Invisible Green

27   PALINODES ———————————————————————

61   Invisible Green

66   *Notes and Intertitles*

67   *About the Author*

PALINODES

28 Splitting

31 A Cloud System
    *Ghost Story — Years Varied as a Bloom of Flowers — A Gust of
    Wind — To Launch a Weather Balloon When the Air is Most
    Calm, 11 a.m. (GMT)*

36 Empire of the Senses
    *The Act of Seeing with One's Own Eyes — Empire of the Senses —
    Sense of the Realm — An Injury to One*

41 Thumb, Throat, Affidavit
    *Waiting for Tear Gas — Today Everything is Connected —
    Thumb, Throat, Affidavit — The Waiting Room*

46 Corrections
    *Sunt lacrimae rerum — If from a City, by Wolves — The Camera
    in the Garden — Corrections*

51 Still Life, Andersonville
    *Windfall Apple — To Make a Hole in a Day as a Nap —
    Still Life, Andersonville*

56 How to Call Back the Dead

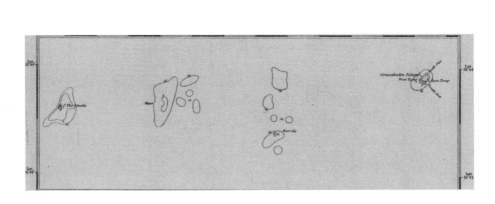

GREENHOUSES, LIGHTHOUSES

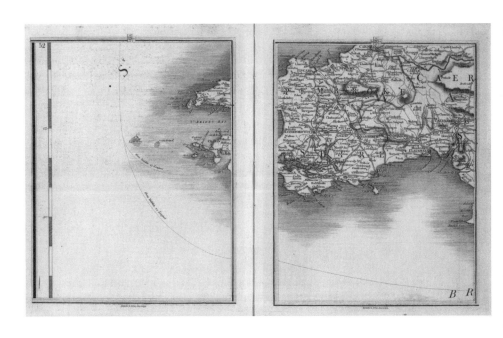

INVISIBLE GREEN

Commanders of vehicles in distress are desired to make their usual signals.
Rooms and bed are provided for shipwrecked seamen…
Dead bodies cast on the shore are decently buried gratis.

The New Seaman's Guide and Coaster's Companion, 1809

In 1772, the twenty-six-year-old violinmaker Henry Whiteside began to build a lighthouse on a pile of rocks twenty miles off the coast of Pembrokeshire, Wales, called the Smalls. His design was unusual; the light perched on top of eight oak piers like the head of a stiff-legged octopus. Rather than making a solid base, Whiteside reasoned, he would let the force of the waves pass through the structure. But when the waves did so, the living quarters swayed violently; one visitor reported that a full bucket of water was half empty by the time he left. The force of the storm made each thing—bucket, glass, stove, table—resonant; it bent the lighthouse, shaping it into an instrument of music.

The violinmaker began his design by setting his compass point at N 51°43'17", W 5°38'47". Then he drew a circle, 3 miles out, the distance of cannon shot and therefore the distance of territorial waters. Another circle, 4 miles out, representing the reach of the Smalls' "pellucid green" beacon: he drew this intermittent light as a series of green dashes. A third circle, 12 miles, thick line: a brighter white light to warn of rocks. A series of concentric circles to represent the ocean, with the lighthouse fixed at the center. But a final circle should be drawn 40 feet out, representing a lighthouse keeper's circuit around the gallery railing in winter. He is at the center of the center; the world comes to him, wrecks itself on his shores.

2

They are out of rations; they are still waiting for lime juice and pickled vegetables. The owners are cheap; the resupply ships are late. Why, then, the rumor that lighthouse keepers "at the last stages of a decline… are prodigiously fat" when they leave their posts? A few years' duty at the Smalls, so they say, wards off consumption, breaks fever, and reverses wasting disease. How can the meanest personalities turn into jolly, good-spirited fellows; how can scrofulous, emaciated men walk in, and corpulent doubles walk out?

As one keeper, formerly a watchmaker, writes, this work is "rusting a fellow's life away." The rotating prisms operate through a clockwork mechanism—he knows how to wind and fix them; the lighthouse is simply a large watch to maintain and repair. But what he belatedly realizes as he is oiling the surface of the gearwork is that he is no longer working on a watch. *He* is the rusted mechanism standing at attention each hour, at twilight and at dawn; in the room full of whale oil and sperm candle, he is the one needing the grease. With no rations left, he eats the oil intended for the candles. Whale oil, rich as cod-liver oil, rich with vitamins, makes the keeper look almost healthy. Food for both stomach and eye. Stink of half-eaten light.

The surface of a glass photograph taken in the village of Solva, where the keepers are based, is pockmarked with white marks that mimic the keepers' vision after repeated exposure to lantern light. These marks seem to float halfway between us and the men on the other side; they are like the translucent deposits that cast shadows as they pass through the eye's vitreous humor. Three keepers gather around an uncomfortable wooden chair for the village photographer. The plate is old and the light unreliable, but none of the men seem particularly fat.

3

The Smalls, it is said, belong to no parish, nor are they within any county; but they are nearest to the Welsh coast, and the inhabitants of the lighthouse are considered as parishioners of Whitchurch.

A Topographical Dictionary of Wales, 1845

4

There is no plant life on Smalls reef, with the exception of a few edible algae: oarweed, channeled wrack, and thongweed. The clothes of the men bringing supplies to the Smalls may have reeked of mackerel and pollock, but the keepers instead smelled the roots of new potatoes growing in soil; they smelled flatness and fences and hips and the idea of territory. Money accumulated in bank accounts back home; as with everything else on the reef, it was difficult to see it grow.

This despite the fact that, for a time, the Smalls was the richest lighthouse in the world. Bringing in £10,510 a year in 1832 for the two widows who owned it, the Smalls charged light-duties from any ship that passed within 12 miles of the rock, whether or not they ever saw its light. "The waters got crowded daily and hourly with ships of mighty tonnage, / and every ton had to pay." So profitable were the abstract movements of ships on a map that the lighthouse's light increasingly became an afterthought. By the time its lease was repurchased by the Crown in 1836, the Smalls lamp shone at just one-eighth the candlepower of public lighthouses.

The sea, once limitless, was getting crowded. As the need for reliable news grew, insurers at Lloyd's commissioned a network of signaling stations in the Irish Channel. A telescope on the Smalls recorded flag semaphores from a passing ship and forwarded these messages to lookout stations on land. The messages ended their travels in London—first in a newsletter originally titled *Ships Arrived at and Departed from several Ports of England, as I have Account of them in London* and renamed *Lloyd's List,* and later, in a wooden room containing a massive bell salvaged from the HMS *Lutine.* When a missing ship was found, the bellman would ring twice; when a ship was confirmed lost, the bellman would ring once, and the members of Lloyd's, known as the Names, would count their losses.

Draw two compass lines south and southwest; draw a third to make the triangle connecting the busiest ports of the transatlantic trade, Liverpool–Lagos–Philadelphia, or Bristol–Falmouth (Jamaica)–New Orleans. At the vertex is the Smalls. One visitor, after seeing a Liverpool port grown rich from slaving ships, described the oak-timber Smalls lighthouse as a "strange wooden-legged Malay-looking barracoon of a building," a barracoon being a type of slatted cage used to temporarily hold slaves who were to be shipped elsewhere. That cargo was sometimes restrained with the use of ropes interwoven with their hair, and typically insured by Lloyd's from "Averages arising by Death and Insurrection." The Names paid out as long as the ship had been properly hulled with copper to keep out tropical woodworms, and more than 10 percent of cargo were killed.

PART I. *Another Name for Center*

Ars Poetica

The new words will be spring and summer.
Poems will continue to pose questions of existence
Though not as probingly as before
Owing to the change in vocabulary
Which stresses the social over the existential
And having over not having. In the new poems,
Endings will be soft, quiet, understated, and
Images will contain recycled content.
Some poems may be made entirely of
Used rubber tires; others, of canvas.
Canvas and *luminous* will be featured;
"Bougainvillea," however, will be replaced
By creeping myrtle and a sense of grace.
Unlike the winter writing, the new writing
Will be light and thrifty. Those lines once
Celebrated for their texture of brocade
Will not be mourned. Instead, they will be
Freed of unnecessary language, as when
Eliminating your job made unnecessary
The word *fired*. That anger, the least complex
Of emotions, thus the hardest to write about,
Succeeds the topic of malaise. Not disdain,
Vengeance, or regret. Just impotent anger
That the new city bears no resemblance
To the old city but keeps the same name.
It is like the Sicilian town of Noto: after an
Earthquake, citizens voted to build a town
Ten kilometers over, also called Noto.
Having lived here all your life,
You can't find your way around.
Water-blue skyscrapers are everywhere,
And there is a luminous river where
Old streets once meandered.

Exposure

Let the blue flower shatter over the medians and I want to draw in the blanks
of your back the moon crescents you can't see and feed you nightshade
or at least eggplants when you are too much in the days, dear, tell me

does daylight corrode your voice or coat everything it touches, lakes,
rivers, white nerves? Then I will tie an oxbow out of your wide meander and
walk down the mission road ringing copper bells when no cars can

hear. We kiss only in black and white since they discontinued
Kodachrome. Have you noticed there is too much sun now:
owing to glass ceilings and the increased saving of daylight time

there is not enough darkness between eye blinks to separate out
the park from its memory, so just say when and I'll start writing
histories of how we met in the playground, how you pushed me down

and asked if I would help you back up. Of the first movie, of covering
your eyes during it, of the first words we spoke, and how few words
we knew because they still lodged in the world, and not yet in us.

History of Pornography

The girl who knocks at your door
to borrow a spoon   then touches
its metal bowl to her lips

the milkweed stalks retting in the
field   their fibers like a neckline
plunging

a shout from the crazy man on
Fresno his mouth   opening
and then still open

Ode, Washington Dulles International Airport

The nineteenth-century town of Willard... was no longer a functioning
municipality by the time construction of the airport began.

Archeological Investigations for NASM Dulles Center

Tomatoes, 1958. Cord of flies
        on thick yellow & red piles of
tomatoes   paid for us

to jack & hitch the old
        schoolhouse onto a
threshing machine

roll it up Willard Road past
        the weatherboard church
its pews & five gravesites removed

for safekeeping   The perforated
        earth filled with
rainwater   ponds, fountains

*

In the south concourse a fountain
        splashed   A policeman
who once worked at the National

Gallery asked do you see
        the monk?   Once he had
pointed it out there was

no mistaking a figure
         of a monk on the brown
and green sculptured surface

"Dulles Airport Is Quiet, Museum-Like"
Washington Post, April 30, 1963

*

How come you're wearing your
         uniform when traveling
did you just finish basic?   Sergeant's

orders   sir   don't want some office
         job   can't wait to deploy
it's all I wanted to do as a kid

can't wait to get out there   sir

*

That night all of us went driving
         on freshly laid tarmac
our voices were beginning

to deepen   most of us believed
         middle age would be the same
process of sinking deeper

into our skin   In moonlight the road
         wasn't a runway yet
& the cornfields not yet a destination.

What Was Rationed

Parachute silk, iron ore, gasoline,
exclamation marks—we used them
to exclaim about the men

who were rationed, too. With two women
for every man, the youngest and most
fertile the first to draw cards,

we spoke shyly, our eyes flashing,
when hearing the words *manpower,
manhunts, mandates, manifestos.*

The time we lived in was exceptional.
To make things last we had to believe this
time would be the last. We bought life

insurance. We learned to worry
if we lived longer than expected.

On Curing Images and Pork

Pernas sallire sic oportet in dolio aut in seria…

Cato, *De agricultura*: CLXII

The tender image is cut thinly
and with the grain.

The tongue removed, it is washed,
then hung in curing rooms.
The strips are turned inward,

away from flies and strangers
and salted with so many layers
of silver nitrate that even the fat

glistens in the light. Spoiled
film smells of vinegar, but good
hygiene will seal it for a decade,

enough to last through times of famine:
when dust closes in, obscuring
the fields, when images are coarse,

when soldiers knock at your door,
summoning you to service.

Cosmos Revealed behind a Dense Curtain of Poppies

And each plant has an equivalent
star in the sky: to read leaves
as pages of starcharts, to navigate by
leaf of acanthus! O lovers, swear not
by the inconstant light of the olive tree.
Feed each other madder root
and take comfort in the thought
your bones grow red: your insides
dyed alizarin of planet Mars to help
find each other in the dark.
Greenhouses, lighthouses. The first
astronomers tended on hands and knees
the soil of the universe, smoothing
away moss, seeding by night.
Now our galaxy has the sixfold
symmetry of ornament on the tower of Alhambra,
shoots curled from stem looping
heaven and earth together. Trace
curlicues and rosettes with your finger.
The chamber sealed off to mortals but
open above, like a poppy.

The Order of Things

Let me tell you the story of the man who always got what he wanted. Knowing what he wished to see, his staff hired shepherds for his mountains, gamekeepers for his forests. It took ever more effort to keep things the same, and soon the whole country worked for him, sending bears meekly to their pits, wolves back to their dens. World as compendium of beasts. Each animal ate the animal one size down, & so on down to cats and mice, but the master was not cruel. To keep the order of things, he would allow the mouse, littlest of all, to climb into the elephant's ear. That was its chance to gnaw the elephant's brain.

Year of Following People

She tells me: I was dead weight on the street.
I couldn't move without other people.
That year, I learned to be pulled forward.
To swing my hips and to walk and to limp.

She tells me: A car followed me in winter.
I moved a block and stopped and
it did, too, keeping its distance, as if each
of us were looking for a missing person,
dragging the river of gasoline and snow.

She tells me: Perhaps following is harder
than discovering. Perhaps the explorers
in Antarctica who followed Scott to their deaths
looked at the emptiness of south
and their bodies turned to compasses,
legs bending south into south.

Gleaners

By custom, we come
last, when grapes are souring
to wine, to gather what is
about to rot. But when we arrived

was the world already in pieces,
everyone to be used up,
taken? Remember my mother
stripping the funeral wreaths,

thinking the dead are dead,
let us keep for a few more days
our carnations.

And now it's almost night. I boil eggs,
roll a warm one slowly
down your back
and it comes to a stop. I say to you

yellow rim of lampshades. Bent
comb cut from horn. Still
you are thought of, tenderly, by others.
So many ways to ruin,
most filled with joy.

Hands and Feet

Now we have come to the part of the book
where touching is encouraged. How sometimes
we hear our grade school teachers
as we read saying, "Keep your hands and feet
to yourself" and begin to feel
what it means to lie next to others,
and not touch them,
even though they have brought home
a fifth of Scotch and a carton of mint
ice cream, your favorite, in the hopes
that you will forget tomorrow's deposition
and rest your hands suggestively
on their shoulders and begin
what Oshima calls the bullfight of love.
But it is not yet nightfall
and still you keep your hands to yourself,
and that stillness is excruciating,
falling asleep like standing
in a subway car surrounded by
people but unable to look at them,
only the occasional spark of body
lurching against body in the dark
to break up the underground
sequence of letters and numbers,
and even that touch prompts a mute
apology and a move down the aisle.
That is another book; this
is the part where touching is encouraged,
where the book must be opened with hand
and foot, separating edible
from inedible, poem from paper shell.

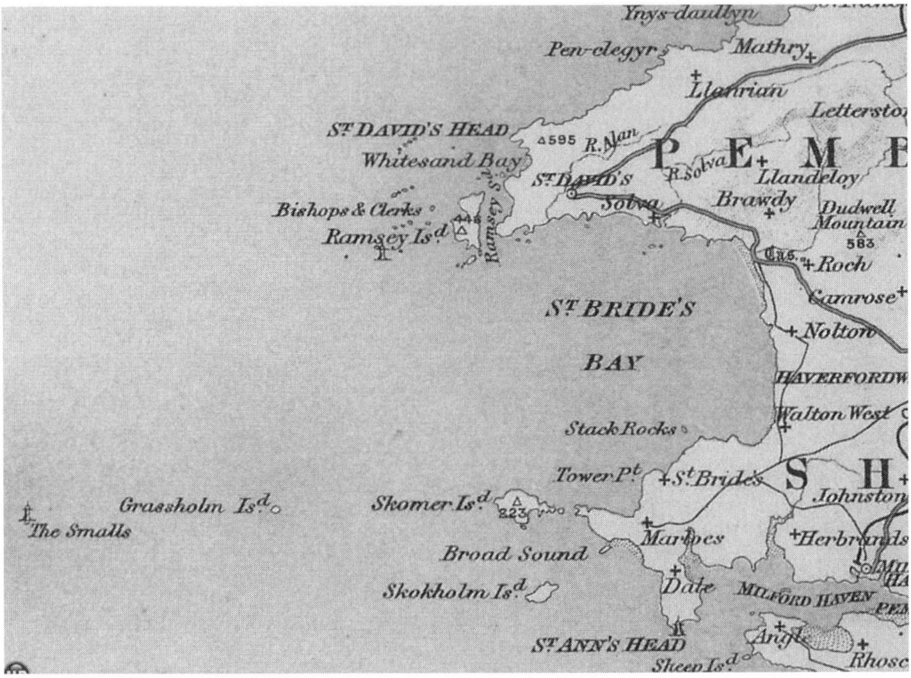

Ynys-daudlyn
Pen-clegyr
Mathry
Llanrian
St. DAVID'S HEAD
Whitesand Bay
595
R. Alan
R. Solva
Llandeloy
St. DAVID'S
Solva
Brawdy
Dudwell
Mountain
583
Bishops & Clerks
Ramsey Isd.
Ramsey Sd.
Roch
Camrose
St. BRIDE'S
BAY
Nolton
Stack Rocks
Walton West
Tower Pt.
St. Bride's
Johnston
Grassholm Isd.
The Smalls
Skomer Isd.
223
Broad Sound
Marloes
Dale
Skokholm Isd.
MILFORD HAVEN
St. ANN'S HEAD
Sheep Isd.

INVISIBLE GREEN

5

In the winter of 1777, Whiteside was called back to reinforce the structure, which had heaved dangerously in the first months after its completion. Caught in a storm lasting two weeks, and with supplies running out, he sat down at his desk and wrote a letter, then made two more copies. He folded each letter inside a bottle and placed each bottle inside a cask with the words "Open this and you will find a letter" painted on the surface.

Smalls, February 1, 1777. *Sir,* —

Almost any weather
you would come to
  seek us as promptly as possible

at some part of the tide-
  house. In a most melancholy manner

I have no need to tell you more,
  you will comprehend

Our distress, H. Whiteside.

The first cask washed ashore in Galway; the second was found by a fisherman in St. David's; but the third arrived in a creek almost directly below the lighthouse's agent. It was not the first message in a bottle ever sent, but it was the first that received a response.

Before the Smalls incident, tar-sealed flasks had once contained what one of Victor Hugo's narrators described as "wills of men in despair, farewells cast to fatherland, revelations of falsified logs, bills of lading, and crimes committed at sea, legacies to the crown, etc.... the black cabinet of the ocean." The ocean may have stood in for a higher power, but it was the power of a bureaucrat, one who inventories and silently files away each complaint into its drawers. The religious wrote to repent; the nationalists, to greet their country; the practical, to finalize business affairs.

We were surprised—

since that time we have not been able to keep
      any temporary light

For want of oil and candles
      make us murmur and think
we have been forgotten.

Ed. Edwards, G. Adams, J. Price.

The cask found in Galway washed ashore two months after it was sent. The mayor mailed a copy of the letter back to its sender, changing the cask into a time capsule. How did Whiteside react in March, after receiving a copy of his own plea for help? Given a chance to have such a conversation, what could you say to your older self? During a storm in 1830, the keepers again sent a cask into the ocean, asking for rescue, but the contents of that message are not recorded. Perhaps this was because, its having worked once, they had come to expect it would work again.

Whiteside's party did not doubt that "whoever takes up this will be so merciful" as to rescue them. They did not doubt that ocean currents would bring their words to the attention of a stranger any more than they doubted the presence of invisible ships passing by who must have seen them. For a few weeks, they had been overcome by a temporary feeling of limitlessness, of transcending the boundaries of the self—not just feeling a connection to all things but feeling as if one *is* the center that connects each part of the map. Psychologist Romain Rolland could not have known of the Smalls when, describing these symptoms to Freud in 1927, he diagnosed its sufferers with "oceanic feeling."

6

To prepare them for their first immersion in the ocean, upper-class women were instructed to dump buckets of water on their heads. There were also ways to protect a person from the sea, among them a thick woolen bathing dress or, when that became indecent, woolen trousers. The bathing machine, invented in 1735 and in wide use by the nineteenth century, would immerse a bather to a depth of twenty centimeters, just deep enough to get a feel for the ocean.

For the men and women who had graduated from the bathing machines on St. Bride's Bay, the Smalls seemed to offer a genuine sense of risk. Sir John Henry Scourfield, MP for Pembrokeshire, penned a ditty (sung to the tune of "Here's to the Maiden of blushing sixteen") about an expedition aboard a ship inauspiciously named the *Quail*:

> Let us go out to sea, for its stupid to sail
> In the limits of the harbour and river;
> . . . .
> Nothing appals,
> Enterprise calls,
> Off we must go on a cruise to the Smalls.

Seeking the limitlessness of the sea, the seafaring party's faces quickly turned blue, yellow, and green as they heaved their lunches into the ocean and waited out the squall on nearby Grassholm Island. Finally the *Quail*'s crew admitted defeat: "people command / A far finer view of the sea from the land."

The Smalls were good for another cheap thrill. In 1800, Thomas Griffiths, a keeper stationed on the lighthouse, died by accident. Unable to flag down a passing ship, the other keeper, Thomas Howell, worried he would be blamed for Griffiths's death. Accordingly, he constructed a coffin from the wooden bulkhead of the living room and lashed it with rope to the outside of the gallery wall. With the passing ships noticing nothing wrong with the light, it was three months before he was relieved. As a result of the trauma Howell experienced while living with a corpse, British lighthouses have had three keepers stationed on them, a strict rule kept until automation in the 1980s.

Though Griffiths is real, his death continues to be told and retold until it becomes fiction, with each teller lingering over each gory detail: the coffin bursting open to reveal a partially decomposed arm waving in the wind; the bottle of rum that may have lured Griffiths to his lethal tumble over a metal railing; the arguments between Thomases younger and older in the public houses of Solva; the hair white with fright when Howell was finally relieved and sent to the madhouse. But these stories are ways of giving a frisson not unlike that of dipping one's toe in cold water for a few seconds. In each story, there is always a beginning, middle, and end.

What is untellable is a sense of time that is monochrome: the flatness of the sky, the small rain that is starting but not yet rising to the level of a gale, the wind that opens onto more wind. Woodcocks, larks, starlings, and blackbirds. The pools left behind in the rock on a spring midafternoon, when tides are at their lowest. A sense that one's vision is being tested when looking at the sea's edges. On the horizon, ship and bird and fish and the idea of north are as interchangeable as the soft forms on the bottom of the optometrist's chart. Difficult as it is to look at the horizon for long periods of time, a determined looker can catch that moment of pure chance known as a green flash. Shot/reverse shot: around sunset, for a fraction of a green second, the horizon looks back.

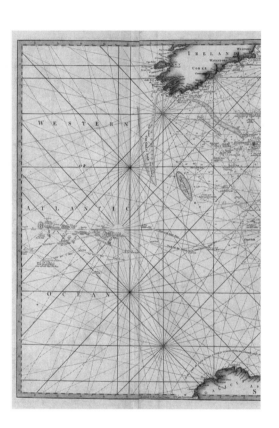

PART II. *Palinodes*

Splitting

I am giving you curtains, kitchen utensils, furniture, photographs, the last word, with each giving I can lessen the amount of me that needs to be forgiven, we exchange rocks with holes drilled in them to mean Now we are incomplete again, now I am showing you the *Nuremberg Chronicle,* these blank pages for the present, sandwiched between Genesis and Revelation, the scribe calculating just enough space for six generations' worth of present. Is that how we reserve space for each other? I remember the moment we stopped believing in the end of the world. We set out for Mexico but got only as far as Los Angeles, city of angels, my love.

*

We set out for Mexico but got only as far as Los Angeles, city of angels, the beach resorts done for the year, the sea churned to butter. We stacked chairs, shot pool in the back. They don't believe in the end of the world here, not where the water laps at our feet. Enrico Fermi took bets on whether the earth would survive the atom blast, whether the atmosphere would ignite and burn for months. Whoever won the bet was a pessimist about his job. That beautiful light, visible all the way from here: the blind able to see again.

*

That beautiful light, visible all the way from here: we won't go to the desert this year and see it. Nor will we see seeds swollen by flash floods and the wildflowers spring out, not just one or two but whole carpets of desert verbena, aster, the hairy caterpillars as long as our hands crawling on them. No yellow and purple mountains in the distance. Not the shape of each body turning in the dark, trying to find the limits between tent, inside, outside. We'll hear about the desert this year as we drive separately down streets smelling of eucalyptus.

*

We drive separately down streets smelling of eucalyptus, the reason being bad city planning, since eucalyptus imported to grow quickly also dies quickly. The king decreed that eucalyptus trees be planted, trees that would last his life span and his life span only. When he died the universe and its earthly representations were to die too, the palace and garden shaped like Mount Meru, the royal staff, his queen, their sons. But who would sweep away the eucalyptus pips? You told me they are the leftovers of memory: they survive the end of the world.

*

You told me they are the leftovers of memory: the bas-reliefs that took a century to carve, when people still believed in slowness. When walking west to east, each foot is an hour of time, and each toe is a minute. And a few hundred miles over to the state line is a life. I am leaving you for the airport, a leaving we practiced every month. The elevated train rocks back and forth in the morning light. Below, the roofs of houses communicate secretly with the heavens, with laundry lines, carrier pigeons, and radio antennas. The body has meridians and channels of energy, too, our bodies expanding outward by touching, the slowest way to reach the world, bending toward each animal, doubling, splitting.

A Cloud System

SHE.

> A breathing image
> made in likeness to me,
> made out of air,
>
> and he thinks he has me,
> but has a useless seeming,
> wrapped in clouds.

> (Euripides, *Helen*)

CHORUS.

> And yet we mostly
> describe times of weather:
>
> the first organ was an air pump &
> the cold winter a screen
> for seeing breath. Your two bodies,
>
> a cloud system,
> hollowed, connected by air.

Ghost Story

> Who was more beautiful?

SHE.

> We resembled each other like
> photographs of clouds:
>
> she the minor version
> of me, her face mirroring me,
> but slowly, inexactly.
>
> The only other time I have felt like this:
>
> when young, I met Anna from
> the next town over. That evening
> I went to the typewriter and typed
> ANNA IS MY RIVAL.
>
> Anna and I,
> two horses drinking from the same river,
> one always upstream from the other.
>
> If only the disaster of adolescence
> had kept us together,
> now that all of you have rivals,
> and I have only this copy of me.
>
> I had not yet learned to be beautiful.
> This was not a true story yet.

Years Varied as a Bloom of Flowers

CHORUS.

> When your new wife whispers
> secrets to a tree, which tree does she hollow?
> How does she shape a listening duct
>
> like the mushroom called wood ear,
> a flared mouthpiece for her lips to fill?
>
> What was so terrible that she sealed
> mud into the hole?

HE.

> Why is it that sometimes, listening
> to you, I can hear the sound of a radiator
>
> breathing steam in a cold room?

A Gust of Wind

MESSENGER.

> Your wife is gone!
> Into the folds of the ether,
> raised up high, invisible.

> (Euripides, *Helen*)

HE.

> Coming home to a home
> ransacked,
>
> the bedsheets had turned into
> kites, a door moved on its hinges,
> and so many things that year
> made light and paper-thin,
>
> as if the wind had taken away
> my belonging, and so nothing
> could be blamed except the evil
>
> that, in some countries,
> they call by name:
>
> tramontana, meltemi, Santa Ana.

To Launch a Weather Balloon When the Air Is Most Calm, 11 a.m. (GMT),

after Nanette Hosenfeld,
National Weather Service, Salt Lake City

is to see the belt of ether all around you:
clouds at ground level, ice falling out of a clear sky,

before it thickens or becomes malevolent,
swelling thousands of balloons to house size

as they photograph the air, not part of the air
but in chorus and above it. We fill the balloons

with gas in the shelters, we hold their necks
like horns as we pass them through the opening

of the dome roof to the outside of seeing, outside
of the outdoors, though they still sound, though they

can be located, though they fall, over there,
in the mountains, in creeks or ravines, postage-paid,

past bursting, crated and marked Return to Sender.
Some have been found as far as two hundred

miles down the interstate, the farthest point
imaginable that might still include us.

Empire of the Senses

When the rain ended we put on waxed jackets
and drove down the road, looking

for the pipe break that left the earth
sunken and loose. A tree fell

into the water; its yellow leaves flashed
like bright hair left in the sink;

an eddy swept its remains underground.
Our own feet balanced on the basin

edge, and beneath the floating world,
we saw dark wells connected by channels,

cisterns. New land. We insisted we were
the first to lay eyes on it.

The Act of Seeing with One's Own Eyes

As you can see,
the warp and weft of flesh is unwoven
starting with the seam of the neck;

then, the shears move through
the bolt of cloth stretched over bone
frames to reveal ruptured pipes

starved of oxygen, a purple-white
basin of spoiled meat. Son, to recap,
until you are seventeen, there is no touching

the sticky joinery of a woman's body;
when viewing lustful pictures
if your body is filmed with sweat imagining
each layer of clothes peeled off

to reveal the depths underneath,
remember the zipper of the dress
is the zipper of cold skin pulled open,

the cold room unlocked by a surgeon's light.

Empire of the Senses

Love, the back of your
mouth is delicate as
mushrooms, caves,

or even moths that come out
at night after painting sugar
on tree bark, feathery,

blanched and translucent
from flashlights. Had I
a hundred tongues yours

would be the kindest and
most radiant: the last
time I saw anything shine

like your gums was at
a pond encircled with
cattails and coarse-tipped

grasses on which beetles
climbed, hard-shelled
and bright as hammers.

Sense of the Realm

Curling your fingers
around a flashlight's
knurled grip, you said
I want you to look at me,

and pressing its lamp on,
you pushed and twisted
the barrel inside,

and the center of your sex
illuminated like a greenhouse
at night.

When we returned to the small
darks of plaster and bedsheets,

I had a sense of the realm
looking back at me;

I walked outside
and the chestnut flowers
were more alive than I could ever be:
the air thick, rotting with seed.

An Injury to One

In some tales an injury
shows up on the body of a statue
in a temple, the serpentine
wake from a dagger shunted,
as if pain could be transported
to the body of another. Perhaps this is why
you avoid me in the middle of the night.
You are afraid pain itself
might develop a way to communicate.

Once, after a bad fall, your hand slit open,
you found a diagram online
and did the sutures yourself, black thread,
liquor, perforating the hand as if to be
outside of and still yourself.
And you show me this knowing
how much your skin, still puckered
near the thread and blue at the edges,
makes me want to touch it,
to reach inside and find—

Do you remember the girl
whose neck was attached
by a ribbon? Who wants to reach
inside the marvelous? Who is the first
to unwrap the ribbon, and who is
left behind, watching?

Waiting for Tear Gas

1. You were holding on to the barrier with one of your hands and he came up and told you to take your hand off.

2. Your hand remained there. He made you withdraw your hand by hitting the rail right next to it.

3. When you leaned it again on the rail, he smashed it with full force. The thumb stayed connected to your hand, as if attached by ribbons.

Zhivka Valiavicharska, November 20, 2009

In our dreams the picket lines
were picket fences. In our dreams
you could run your hands
between two halves

of the city. Close enough
to taste the mustard greens
cooking in the neighbor's kitchen,
your mouth filling with tears.

You could even follow the line as it curved
like parentheses through the streets
and see everything it held back

the way a dam holds the lake behind it,
or a calendar year keeps at bay
the years piling up before it.

Today Everything Is Connected

By a single principle: guilt by association.
For this reason, when it is revealed
That we sometimes have trouble distinguishing
Between the noise and the shape of things,
The hand from the fist, the gestures of love
From the gestures of waiting, it means that
Anyone may be accused at any time.
Simply raise your index finger and point
Across the room and someone will come over

To take your order. Although it is not polite
I am going to accuse the sun of failing to rise
During off-hours. I will accuse those handing out
Lemons and onions of asking for it.
I will even accuse myself of conspiring
To sell sadness as a small, mysterious gift.
The only animal you can trust is the woodpecker
Who points repeatedly to its tree and says
Each time You are here. My love, you are here.

Thumb, Throat, Affidavit

At this point your credit score
will be helpful. Turn in your old pictures
and walk the way you have always walked,
feet turned out, heels light as oars.
Request letters of reference from those
proper to you,
those who speak for you when you are held,
speechless. The grocer finds evidence you once
stole candy, and in doing so,

proves your existence,
young, unafraid of the law, desired. Another
remembers the tree house that grows
silver with age, lumber turning back to forest.
Have you heard the phrase Lend me your hands?
Your parents, when they were still in love,
learned each other's signature. Angle after loop,
teaching one another how to become another.

The Waiting Room

Say the cops don't come.
Say you never went to

Say that before a certain time
        even your double has been expunged.

You imagine it as a cellar
that holds a single lightbulb,
        a record turning. A fado
pours out its lament:

Until I see you again, there will be
        no seeing, only a sense of light
        and dark from the next room.

The hallway
        nearly ablaze from her voice.
Until I see you again. The windows

don't open anywhere but an old stairwell.

Sunt lacrimae rerum

After the house fire
we asked him what he lost
but all he said was
there is a poignancy
to things they cry
when burned even bricks
let out water somehow

Each day we hid one
thing to see if he noticed
we took the acorns from the
oaks we caught the
squirrels as they
buried acorns

then the building inspector
hid the roofs too
and we asked him what he missed
what he said was
the month between
September and November
is a hole he made a gesture
with his hand he touched
his fingertip to his thumb

and his house was a leaf
curling in on itself
a sky sky leaf

If from a City, by Wolves

Sometimes I am like the traffic
accident that causes other
accidents, the onion
cut next to your heart. Sometimes I
am the first magnet, the new guy
at the door who, six times out of ten,
will cause your son to burst
into tears when first meeting me.
He'll run away because, at two,
he's old enough to tell that I
am the heaviness holding up
the Bay Bridge, the water
in the salt solution that means
I am forever the solvent
and you the solute, the onion
moving against the heart. Some-
times the onion and other times the heart,
I look at the weeping willow
in your yard and begin to think
If even trees weep then the world
is full of tears. Your son and I,
traffic and accident. Beside and oneself.

The Camera in the Garden

My mother who used to put
a photograph of a boy under
where the water hose drips
in order to be in two

places at once tells me
she used to watch his
face turn gray and old
until he seemed capable
of love: she did it again

with other boys not just
that one and they
still lie in the garden
talking to each other
about the woman who

visited every night
to water them when
even the animals that howl
could not find water

Corrections

When out walking, you may find
faces frozen under the lake.
They are a trick of light; a real face
would never remain fixed and
unmoving for so long. Thousands
of muscles cause faces to undulate
constantly, like kites in the wind.
Do not sing to them, prod them,
or walk out over them.
The faces only call to us because,
as ice ages and becomes clearer,
they gradually come into focus.
As in an accident, better to look away
than to think of the book of memory
thrown in the lake, its pages curling
outward, as if some hand had
peeled them apart as carefully
as the wings of rare insects
and mounted them onto glass.
How silent it must be down there.
We have sent pumps out
to dissipate the faces. The pumping
will commence soon.

Corrections

Newark, New Jersey, is not America's renaissance
city, as I wrote previously; that is Pittsburgh.
Newark is dying and has a bleak future.
A recent poem implies that I am lonely.
I am not; my mouth is just shaped that way,
small and sad-looking. And due to an editing error,
our dog is listed as our pack leader. This is a mistake;
our leader is the president, who governs
with the consent of the people. But if even people
are mistaken? Then I believe in amnesty.
Each side to marry their enemy, ghosts to live
peacefully among us like months waiting
to turn thick and flush with moisture. Calendar
and chronicle annulled. Unlink names from
their dead and return names to where they
may be changed and forgotten and used again.
And faces? Faces, too. Let the oceans be milk-white
with the accumulated light of old photographs.

Still Life, Andersonville

This is not a true story;
you did not board the wide-bodied jets;
you did not go to New York in September:

instead, when the plane returned to red earth,
something hard in the sky
loosened,

the moment a mark,
an extra comma in the conversation,
a pause in asking where you
had landed,

and, not hearing a response from
the brick walls and old grates,
turning to the birds,
the yellow jackets, turning to them
to ask.

Everyone knew the new words
would be about loss,
but in the meantime, there was such

abundance: the low price of gasoline,
birds on a field of dropped
fruit. I became hungry and washed

my face in the sink's cold water.
The smell of new bread in the oven,
of someone else's soap while bathing;
at dinner, my host asked
for salt, reached for it, then

drove off, saltshaker still in hand. Passed
a sheriff on the road not heading
anywhere. What is a sheriff in a world

of soldiers? On the pocket of a starched
blue shirt, his gold six-pointed star,
palm-heavy, shaped like a toy.

Windfall Apple

That month the road was apple trees and the air was apple trees, too.
>   There was nothing that was not apples. Sex was

ripe and round and plucked things and what we were doing was an act
>   of generosity. Picking up the fallen, eating, etc.

As if after a year of fork & knife we had been allowed to take
>   with our hands, and had just learned how to use them.

The hand has rules: everything that is loose may be gleaned.
>   A hand counts and gathers the weight of a single apple,

returning over and over to the moment of having.

To Make a Hole in a Day as a Nap

Divide time like a piece of fruit:

morning will be the flesh, afternoon the seeds,
night the pith of day.

To pull apart until you hear others
counting their breath;

to make clocks out of water and clocks
out of honey and paint and dandelions.

To time the bitter of tea as it
fades from our tongues,

to place an apple next to another
and start this cycle of nearness

which we call a clock,
ripening.

Still Life, Andersonville

For the first time we did not count the days
        thick with the texture of cream or wax. The train

did not quake at 2 a.m. and our windows did not
        knock on their joins. We did not hear the wheels

carrying wheat from the Midwest dried and bound
        in sheaves, West Texas crude glistening in metal drums,

and when it stopped the city was not us but we
        were the freight of the city. On TV, in the distance,

people were dying. But now we could hear the space of
        prairie between us, the sound of what painters call

nature morte, dead nature. With air swollen to a husk, a stillness
        settled over our beds at night, over the apples, unwanted,

ripening, stacked by the thousands in the packer's yard.

How to Call Back the Dead

Don't mumble. Speak clearly:
Parliament of the missing.

Leave the windows slightly ajar:

now brush them with your picture resins,
chloride of gold +
pure crystallized honey +
beaten eggwhite

leave our glassy ransom in the dark.

Leave and in the morning
call to us. The flies

arrive suddenly: our bodies smelling
sweet-sour, our tongues stinging.

Paint over us with layers of praise.

Oh! how fast you call me back,
though I have settled, already,
into the woods where
deer and asphodel
do not look like you. Everyone is

dead here & we each have instincts
that will take years to scent out.
Now I know what it is to be startled,
to brush a branch, to look backward,
and not see anyone following. Only

in the dream you tell: Someone sets his hands
on the slope of your shoulders.
You lift your arms up (wings
of a corkscrew) and now he takes your
torso and turns you and you remember

how light you feel, light as the time
you tried to get a good look at yourself,
straining, practically spinning, to see—
Your lovely back: rows of muscle, sinew.
Tapestries hung from girders.

Not the cemetery where you once listened against headstones.
Not aboard a ship or an island,

no weapons left out on the porch: no pitchforks, no guns.
Nothing loose, nothing heavy, no rocks out of place.

Not against, not again, not final,
not yet. Just a clean, well-watered place at the side of the road,

a suburb lined with elm trees, verdant from the sun.
"Somewhere in between Paris and Alençon,

a half-drunk barber used to invite soldiers who were passing
on the road to come and have a free shave in his shop."

How thin the walls are
between belonging and not belonging,
a drum stretched across
so much space. One hears echoing
on the street. Children dress
up like us and chase
each other with guns.
And when they press their ears against me,
on the other side the birds do
not sing and the dogs do not
bark in my language.

INVISIBLE GREEN

7

In October 1812, the ocean around the Smalls was a color known then as invisible green, a green so dark it is mistaken for black if not under direct light. Invisible green was also the recommended shade for painting garden fences so as to blend them into the surrounding landscape. As the poet William Mason wrote: "The limits, as it were, retire from the view, and use and beauty… are now indistinguishably united again."

When the green waves reached thirty-two feet, the height of the lightroom, the men, frightened, broke the glass to have a way to swim out. (The light spilled out of the glass as they went; the light became an invisible layer of paint under the water.) Whiteside didn't see the problem; he responded that the "house would have been somewhat leaky the windows being broken." By then, age sixty-six and married to the daughter of the Old Ship Inn's proprietor, his attention had turned toward his own house, the trees uprooted in his own garden.

The Fresnel lens that eventually replaced the old lamp gave off a hard light. As in a Barbara Stanwyck film, each crisp shadow on a keeper's face became visible. A man disappeared behind a doorway; fragments emerged—the thick neck, the hands, the brass buttons on his double-breasted blazer. The rest engulfed by dark, as if under water. Rather than the "pellucid green" light of the original design, a beehive of glass draped around a glowing center. Three flashes of the Smalls like a flashbulb going off three times. The lantern room sparkling like a recently stolen necklace.

Today the invisible comes to us mostly in the form of cell phone reception and radar guns. The invisible green sea that historians speak of is not the green of now, just as we are unsure whether the wine-dark sea was black or more the color of clotted blood. We know only that it is dark, as the dark appears on a winter afternoon: a surprise.

"*Milford,* 22 April—The brig *London Packet,* Poyntz, of Bristol, sailed from hence for Tortola on 16th inst; on the evening of the 17th, Captain Roberts, of the

Freeling Post Office Packet, on his passage from this to Waterford, near the Smalls Light House, picked up a water cask and small scuttle, both marked *London Packet;* also a seaman's check, and a box with books, but in taking up the box, the bottom and books dropped out. There was a signal flying on the Smalls Lighthouse, but as it was nearly dark, Captain Roberts could not communicate, nor has there been any communication with the Smalls and shore since the 4th instant, so that it is conjectured there may be some wrecked mariners on it."

The estate at Llanunwas was notorious for setting false lights on its cliffs above Solva, a few miles from the reef. Land and sea, optically reversed: imitating a lighthouse was once the coast's second industry, its unspoken economy. If a coal fire was too much effort, one could make do with rope yarn soaked in pitch and tar, even a lantern hung from the neck of a mule induced to move slowly. The wreckers waited to rescue the cargo of ships that came to grief. If questioned, they might explain the obvious: the ocean sometimes strips its victims clean, just as the desire for land sometimes exceeds land itself. And if pressed, they would express sympathy for "the wandering mariner, in order to benefit by his misfortunes; [   ] atrocious crimes, coupled [   ] the inhuman perpetrators."

The cask and coal scuttle and the box that fell out of the *London Packet* were jetsam: the fee paid to escape the ship. Had the mariners intended to recover the books they had lost, the books would be termed lagan, that which lies at the bottom of an ocean; otherwise, derelict, that which is abandoned altogether. The woman currently in charge of determining what to do with the books is Alison Kentuck, whose first step toward a career in marine archaeology was excavating Victorian trash from an abandoned hospital at the age of sixteen. Kentuck is also responsible for disposing of any royal fish stranded on British shores: whales, dolphins, porpoises, and sturgeon. During her work, she wears a bright-yellow safety vest with reflective tape and the words RECEIVER OF WRECK emblazoned on the back.

9

... 9 casks of white lead, the 112 cases of English China, the 341 pieces of cloth and also 20 casks of cudbear for dyeing it; 16 hatchets; 45 pipes of linseed oil;

For nearly a century, the most reliable fog signal was a bird colony. The Skerries lighthouse kept a colony of terns as late as 1863; close to it, the South Stack light had gulls so tame they were considered pets by the keepers. Together, the two different birdcries allowed a ship to navigate between two rocks that, in fog, looked like perfect twins. The sounds from the Smalls light consisted of seals barking and gannets from nearby Skokholm Island. You could not navigate too well by these sounds, but at least your fog signals did not risk being eaten by escaped rats. "A cat has been tried / but she preferred birds to rats."

So had explosives been tried, and whistles, gongs, bells, horns, sirens, reeds, and diaphones. Yet the signals continued to disappear. An explosion on land might be heard twenty-five miles away, on the Smalls, but not on a ship three miles away; it was as if the sounds had been swallowed by the ocean, only to reappear in another place entirely. Physicist John Tyndall studied the fog-signal problem on the lighthouse authority's steamship *Irene,* concluding that sound waves were being deflected by "acoustic clouds." His notes on July 3, 1873, read: "The echoes reached us, as if by magic, from the invisible acoustic clouds with which the optically transparent atmosphere was filled." For Tyndall, we were surrounded by a sort of noble ghost "incessantly floating or flying through the air," regally indifferent to our senses, and palpable only in its reflection.

The acoustic clouds gave a plausible if ultimately inaccurate explanation for sounds lost at sea. At heart, though, they were less scientific theory than an expression of faith: that a listener could be found for every speaker, even if the ear of a ghost; that the invisible lines that connected Liverpool and Philadelphia also connected signs and events across two moments in history. That somewhere in the fog was an audience for the concert where the lighthouse was metronome, chamber, and orchestra.

Now, as a signaling station, the Smalls watches for news in the Irish Channel: shipwrecks, lost cargo. But its keepers also listen for fainter signals, such as the buzz of two bumblebees (*Bombus* sp.) recorded as traveling west on the unusually warm July 7, 1955. Or the quail that manages to escape from a hunt on the mainland and spends the month of May 1960 jumping into rock pools. After his shift is over, the keeper takes the quail home, thinking he will raise the lost bird with his chickens. Someone in the lighthouse counts this bird and remembers its call. A quail is lost, and a hundred miles away, as if by magic, it reappears as a chicken.

11

The oak timbers of Whiteside's old structure are gone, but the sense of oak is still there: the new Smalls, a granite structure built in 1861, got its shape when an architect noticed that oaks in the English countryside almost never toppled over or were uprooted by a storm. He designed a granite structure for the Eddystone Rocks that flared at the base and tapered, like an oak trunk, to a cylinder at the top. The new lighthouse on the Smalls is similarly rooted to the ocean, and when a harsh swell makes the whole structure sway, that movement is considered "the healthy elasticity of a living thing." Ocean-oak. Even the stumps of Whiteside's oak legs, now over two centuries old, are slowly turning to stone; the sea salt has petrified their stumps. The only living thing that grows on the rock is itself made of rock.

The Smalls, the first lighthouse to be fitted with the luxury of a flushing toilet, now finds its prized toilet mostly unused; its keepers, like those at other rock lighthouses, are stationed on land, where they keep watch from computer screens. Solar and wind generators silently power a single 35-watt bulb. Rock lighthouses have been automated, and increasingly send out electronic AIS signals instead of fog signals, for the one place a foghorn cannot be heard is the inside of a modern container ship, with its engines running and the captain surrounded by its superstructure. So the foghorns on the Smalls revert to what they have always been, since the time of Whiteside: Reeds and winds. Pipe organs. Musical instruments.

It is said that Whiteside was fond of tuning his fiddle during a storm, that he would go out to the cliffs so that he could capture the wind's pitch. It is also said that his beech-wood violins, which had a sweet and mellow tone, could once be heard all over Solva. Though his violins are gone, one can still go to the cliffs. Below, a wind gusts through the shingle beach and dislodges a few pebbles at a time. The shingles skid against one another, giving off a series of hard clicks, some long, some short.

NOTES AND INTERTITLES

IN PART 1:

"Cosmos Revealed behind a Dense Curtain of Poppies" is from Michael Auping, in *Anselm Kiefer: Heaven and Earth*, exhibition catalogue, 2005.

IN THE PALINODES:

1

Splitting, house, photographs, and film by Gordon Matta-Clark, 1974. The last paragraph of "Splitting" is after Anne Wagner, "Splitting and Doubling: Gordon Matta-Clark and the Body of Sculpture," *Grey Room*, no. 14, winter 2004.

2

"A Cloud System": The translation of Euripides is from Wendy Doniger, *Splitting the Difference: Gender and Myth in Ancient Greece and India*, 1999.
"Years Varied as a Bloom of Flowers": *In the Mood for Love*, a film directed by Wong Kar-Wai, 2000.
"A Gust of Wind": *A Gust of Wind at Eijiri*, a woodcut by Katsushika Hokusai, 1831.

3

"Empire of the Senses": *In the Realm of the Senses*, a film directed by Nagisa Oshima, 1976.
"The Act of Seeing with One's Own Eyes": *The Act of Seeing with One's Own Eyes*, a film by Stan Brakhage, 1971.
"An Injury to One" Is an Injury to All: a union slogan, Industrial Workers of the World.

4

"Waiting for Tear Gas": *Waiting for Tear Gas*, a photographic sequence by Allan Sekula, 1999-2000. Text from George Cicariello-Maher, "Occupy Everything!" *Counterpunch*, November 24, 2009.

6

"To Make a Hole in a Day as a Nap": *To make a hole in a day as a nap*, the subtitle accompanying *Dec. 31, 1996*, a painting by On Kawara, 1966.

7

The last three lines of "Not the cemetery..." quote Emmanuel Levinas, "Wholly Otherwise," trans. Simon Critchley, in *Re-Reading Levinas*, ed. Robert Bernasconi and Simon Critchley, 1991.

Tung-Hui Hu is the author of two previous books of poetry, *Mine* (2007) and *The Book of Motion* (2003). He teaches poetry and media studies at the University of Michigan, where he is an assistant professor of English.

Lannan Literary Selections

For two decades Lannan Foundation has supported the publication
and distribution of exceptional literary works. Copper Canyon Press
gratefully acknowledges their support.

LANNAN LITERARY SELECTIONS 2012

James Arthur, *Charms Against Lightning*

Natalie Diaz, *When My Brother Was an Aztec*

Matthew Dickman and Michael Dickman, *50 American Plays*

Tung-Hui Hu, *Greenhouses, Lighthouses*

Michael McGriff, *Home Burial*

RECENT LANNAN LITERARY SELECTIONS FROM COPPER CANYON PRESS

Michael Dickman, *Flies*

Laura Kasischke, *Space, in Chains*

Deborah Landau, *The Last Usable Hour*

Sarah Lindsay, *Twigs and Knucklebones*

Heather McHugh, *Upgraded to Serious*

W.S. Merwin, *Migration: New & Selected Poems*

Valzhyna Mort, *Collected Body*

Taha Muhammad Ali, *So What: New & Selected Poems, 1971–2005*,
translated by Peter Cole, Yahya Hijazi, and Gabriel Levin

Lucia Perillo, *Inseminating the Elephant*

Ruth Stone, *In the Next Galaxy*

John Taggart, *Is Music: Selected Poems*

Jean Valentine, *Break the Glass*

C.D. Wright, *One Big Self: An Investigation*

Dean Young, *Fall Higher*

For a complete list of Lannan Literary Selections from
Copper Canyon Press, please visit Partners on our website:
www.coppercanyonpress.org

Poetry is vital to language and living. Since 1972, Copper Canyon Press has published extraordinary poetry from around the world to engage the imaginations and intellects of readers, writers, booksellers, librarians, teachers, students, and donors.

WE ARE GRATEFUL FOR THE MAJOR SUPPORT PROVIDED BY:

THE PAUL G. ALLEN
FAMILY FOUNDATION

Lannan

THE MAURER FAMILY
FOUNDATION

NATIONAL
ENDOWMENT
FOR THE ARTS

WASHINGTON STATE
ARTS COMMISSION

Anonymous

Arcadia Fund

John Branch

Diana and Jay Broze

Beroz Ferrell & The Point, LLC

Mimi Gardner Gates

Gull Industries, Inc.
on behalf of William and Ruth True

Mark Hamilton and Suzie Rapp

Carolyn and Robert Hedin

Steven Myron Holl

Rhoady and Jeanne Marie Lee

Maureen Lee and Mark Busto

New Mexico Community Foundation

H. Stewart Parker

Penny and Jerry Peabody

Joseph C. Roberts

Cynthia Lovelace Sears and Frank Buxton

The Seattle Foundation

Charles and Barbara Wright

The dedicated interns and faithful
volunteers of Copper Canyon Press

To learn more about underwriting Copper Canyon Press titles,
please call 360-385-4925 ext. 103

The Chinese character for poetry is made up of two parts:
"word" and "temple." It also serves as pressmark for
Copper Canyon Press.

The poems are set in Perpetua.
Book design and composition by Phil Kovacevich.
Printed on archival-quality paper at McNaughton & Gunn, Inc.